THE FLORIST'S AT MIDNIGHT

THE FLORIST'S
AT MIDNIGHT

Sarah Maguire

CAPE POETRY

Published by Jonathan Cape 2001

2 4 6 8 10 9 7 5 3 1

First published in Great Britain in 2001 by
Jonathan Cape
Random House, 20 Vauxhall Bridge Road,
London SW1V 2SA

Random House Australia (Pty) Limited
20 Alfred Street, Milsons Point, Sydney,
New South Wales 2061, Australia

Random House New Zealand Limited
18 Poland Road, Glenfield,
Auckland 10, New Zealand

Random House South Africa (Pty) Limited
Endulini, 5A Jubilee Road, Parktown 2193, South Africa

The Random House Group Limited Reg. No. 954009
www.randomhouse.co.uk

A CIP catalogue record for this book
is available from the British Library

ISBN 0224062131

Papers used by Random House are natural, recyclable products made from wood grown in
sustainable forests; the manufacturing processes conform to the environmental regulations of
the country of origin

Typeset by Palimpsest Book Production Limited,
Polmont, Stirlingshire
Printed and bound in Great Britain by
Biddles Ltd, Guildford and King's Lynn.

For August

CONTENTS

ACKNOWLEDGEMENTS

Grateful acknowledgement is made to the editors of the *London Review of Books* and *The Times Literary Supplement* in which some of these poems were first published. The title poem was commissioned by Don Paterson and Jo Shapcott for the Salisbury Poetry Festival 1999 and published in *Last Words: New Poetry for the New Century* (Picador). '*Umbellularia californica*' was first broadcast as part of *Works in Progress* on BBC Radio 3, produced by Fiona McLean. 'Winter Solstice' was commissioned for *A Short History of Darkness* and first broadcast on BBC Radio 4. 'African Violet' and 'Rosemary' were first broadcast on *Fine Lines* on BBC Radio 4.

I would also like to extend my deepest gratitude to The Royal Literary Fund and The House at Pooh Corner whose generous financial support saved me from a miserable existence and allowed me to write.

Many thanks to Robin Robertson for editorial skills well beyond the call of duty.

Much love to Andrew, Crispin, Jo, Joe, Nick, Ruth, Sally, Sharon and Veronica. I'd not have survived this without you.

THE FLORIST'S AT MIDNIGHT

Stems bleed into water
　loosening their sugars
　　into the dark,

clouding dank water
　stood in zinc buckets
　　at the back of the shop.

All night the chill air
　is humid with breath.
　　Pools of it mist

from the dark mouths
　of blooms,
　　from the agape

of the last arum lily –
　as a snow-white wax shawl
　　curls round its throat

cloaking the slim yellow tongue,
　with its promise of pollen,
　　solitary, alert.

Packed buckets
　of tulips, of lilies, of dahlias
　　spill down from tiered shelving

nailed to the wall.
　Lifted at dawn,
　　torn up from their roots

then cloistered in cellophane,
　they are cargoed across continents
　　to fade far from home.

How still they are
    now everyone has gone,
        rain printing the tarmac

the streetlights
    in pieces
        on the floor.

ROSEMARY

The small sprig crumbled in my pocket
tucked inside my old blue jacket
hung up in the closet the whole winter long.

Plucked from the tall bush by the garden gate –
the glaucous spikes,
the sheer blue flowers just starring into bloom.

Even now, the faint, insistent scent –
a slim tincture of openness,
stringent and clear.

No one saw me leave the garden.
No one knows.
And now, the tendril powders in my hand.

GARDENIA

One lopsided, scorched-brown bloom
then refusal on the kitchen windowsill.

Symmetrical and silent, the glossy pools
of leaves bisected into light and shade,

the nubbed buds stubborn,
green as leaves, crouching in the foliage.

Faking patience, the north light is
luminous, whitening as the spring comes on.

Once I turn my back, the flowers untwist
in hours, fattening with odour,

with the heady heat of flawless whiteness.
The carved, curved geometry of the blooms

more lucid than hallucination.
As simple, as thoughtless as a bruise.

UMBELLULARIA CALIFORNICA

My lodestar,
the headache tree,
has plotted this garden –

the shy silver birch
placed in its shadow,
the ornamental waterfall

just so,
making fake waves
on a beach of big pebbles,

one lone mallard
motoring
the Japanese pond.

Decades ago
its slip
crossed the Atlantic,

tough thongs of roots
keeling down
through dark loam.

Now, once more, I am
flat out
on a slab of oolitic limestone,

absorbing the dusk
leaking blue
through its tall net

of branches,
the three-pronged trunk
a plumbline of evening,

those swarming
black leaves
fingerpainting the sky.

What unguents beat
through its
heartwood?

What alchemy
forges
those naphthalene leaves? –

slim, dangerous bay leaves:
torn
they let go

an odour
as heady as camphor,
tightening the third eye,

a poultice for the fury
of the mind
drawn into one point.

Once done,
the dusty brown scales
are shoaled

into hiding,
or taken by the wind
tick tick along the path.

Even the flowers
are secret: pale
yellow umbels

show at the cusp
of winter,
way out of reach.

Cynosure reeling me in
since my teens,
my life

graven
in that rough bark
furrowed like the seabed

pleated by waves,
the history and memory
of all these sunsets

transformed into cambium,
laid down
in rings.

I come here
not for a cure
(analgesic, demulcent)

but for a witness,
for the process
of a map.

AFRICAN VIOLET

Tender and cautious,
shipped north across continents,

the African violet
blooms into mildness –

seeking the equinox,
patient, till day

balances the night.
Hirsute secret hoods

ease back
the gauzy, veiled flesh

to a star of opening mauve,
pierced at the heart

with sheer gold –
pollen sacs hidden and swollen.

Neglected in winter
the furred leaves fur with dust,

with trails of lint,
with a lost web going nowhere.

Little succulent overlapped and stacked plates
the leaves rosette from their roots;

crimson of the vulnerable underleaves
intimate as a mouth.

Plunged under water
the flat leaves are aglitter –

small cells full of air
picketing the hairs,

till jostled
they seethe aloft,

freckling the meniscus
with burst.

Snapped, the rich veins ooze
their glossy ichor;

laid onto loam
the tiny adventitious roots

furl through the soil,
shaking a new plant free within weeks.

HIBISCUS

I have no idea what is coming
   as I take the hand of a perfect stranger
      as I'm taken through the streets of Marrakesh.

The exhilaration of trust.
   The exhilaration of risk,
      of balance –

of balancing on the back of his Vespa like a teenage lover,
   my hands gathering his jacket at the waist,
      learning how to give round corners,

forgetting the crush of traffic from nine directions,
   forgetting the chaos at crossroads,
      my cheek now on his back,

the disinterested city
   open before us,
      passing me by.

We loop away from the Djemaa el Fna,
   we loop away from snake-charmers, pet monkeys, jugglers,
      beggars, fortune-tellers, water-sellers,

tagines and harira and brochettes,
   from strings of white lightbulbs,
      from the scent of burnt charcoal

burning the night up all night long,
   we loop away from the slipper souk and the silver souk,
      from the Koutoubia Mosque,

from the Kasbah Mosque and the El Mansour Mosque,
   from the palaces, all the palaces,
      from the medina which now I will never walk through,

from the gardens closed for the night.
  We loop away from that one huge bud of hibiscus –
    madder red, almost cerise –

that is, at this minute, coming full into bloom,
  opening its impossibly crimson throat wide open,
    now, in the dark, before midnight, exactly,

that one hibiscus bloom,
  the one I could have gazed at, gazed into,
    eye to eye

drinking in its throat,
  its scarlet throat,
    its stigma and stamens just risen,

pushing from the petals,
  out of the petals into the night,
    vulnerable and slender and scarlet,

the anthers swollen, dusted yellow with pollen.
  That one hibiscus blooming in a garden
    I will now neither visit nor know

– while I weave through traffic with a stranger,
  our words swept up by the wind
    and thrown off into the night.

I am balancing.
  I am laughing.
    I am lost in the suburbs of Marrakesh.

The city is a tent.
  The city is a rose tent.
    The low rose buildings pleated together,

the castellated walls smoothed out of mud,
    the wide boulevards spinning off into the desert,
        streetlights painting the rose walls

with slashes of amber and bronze,
    white streetlights,
        high up, threading the boulevards,

spinning them into the night, into the desert.
    We are camping in the desert.
        In a desert scented with orange-blossoms,

with the first flush, the young flush of the earliest jasmine,
    with date palms to guide us,
        with date palms pushing up higher

than the rose-coloured buildings,
    higher than the haze of charcoal and spiced food,
        their huge crowns crowning Marrakesh,

their stately crowns swaying in the breeze
    that shifts down from the mountains.
        And we sway through the city, bending and circling,

passing all these people I will never greet –
    the men in white shirts talking on corners,
        the women in djellabas going home with the shopping,

the women in djellabas riding on mopeds,
    headscarves like banners
        streaming behind them,

four boys in an alley playing football
    with a football with a puncture,
        and the old man in the kiosk

where he picks up the key,
    while I straddle the moped
        shifting warm metal from right thigh to left thigh,

absorbing the glances,
    the half-curious glances,
        shot at a white women in this end of town.

Not much further.
    The rose buildings are concrete, closer together.
        We lift the bike up under the stairs

then climb them in darkness,
    hand in hand, feeling the walls,
        right up to the roof

to a room loaned for the night;
    a room with a mattress and a candle and a radio
        (a radio which, in Arabic then French,

will murmur of disasters just out of my grasp).
    When he leaves me to piss
        I go to the window

to map out this journey, to find Marrakesh,
    and I pull back the shutters,
        the stiff slatted shutters –

and there, between the slats and the glass,
    balanced on less than one inch of sill,
        is a bird's nest.

A bird's nest woven of a filigree of fine straw
    and cardboard
        and small curled grey feathers,

with two eggs,
    two cream and brown-speckled eggs,
        nestled together in the cup of the nest,

warm and oval and whole.
    I watch these eggs until I know them.
    I watch the lights of Marrakesh

high above the buildings rise up to the stars.
    I watch Marrakesh
        through this dusty windowpane,

through a window with a crescent of glass
    snapped off at the root.
        Then I close my eyes

and ease back the shutters.
    I return to a room I will never return to
        and I kneel on the mattress.

All night the radio loses the station
    to a whisper of static,
        the soft cry of crossed songs.

CLOVES AND ORANGES

My souvenir of Taliouine
was oranges: three oranges
to bring this place to mind.
They glowed like pumpkin-lanterns
in the garden in the dark

on the last tree by the house;
their luminous skin
aromatic and oily and waxed.
Not quite oranges,
some cross-breed grafted on –

a scar on the trunk
where the damaged cambium
had swollen with healing.
The glossy, oval leaves.
The plump fruits secret in the leaves.

I woke that night
in my white-painted tower
with its three small windows
and knew I'd not come back:
the huge stars hammered

in the sky,
the Atlas mountains folded in sleep,
the river bed
rustling with bamboo.
I will never come back.

In London I ate one of the oranges,
split one with a friend,
left the other in the bowl.
Oh, they were sharp!
like hybrid grapefruit,

too tart for eating.
But the third
I studded full of cloves.
Each tiny crucifixion
a fizz of oil through the skin,

as, pore by pore,
I pressed the clove-nails in,
till the whole globe
bristled with small woody buds.
I looped a ribbon round it

and hung the final orange
from a nail.
Memory is smell.
Next winter,
night by night,

I'll loosen one clove,
then the next.
I'll burn them,
one by one,
till the fruit is bald and gone.

JASMINE IN YEMEN

In the Friday prayers' gridlock
a man with a *djambia*
and a cheek full of *qat*
casts a garland of jasmine
through the shattered car window.
Luck and friendship.
A heady necklace of deaths
looped round my shoulders,
the sharp pungent blooms
fighting the tang of exhaust
and spent oil,
the funk of blown meat
from a plague of pink plastic bags.
Soon the flowers will bruise and fall.
A circle of string left hanging on a doorknob.
Lost petals where I strayed
from the balcony to the bedroom.

CHINAMPAS

The Floating Gardens of Xochimilco
are all that remains
of the wild surmise
of Hernán Cortés
when he first saw Mexico –

Tenochtitlán
the great city of canals
of islands woven from grasses and mud
balanced on willow roots
reaching right down to the pith of the lake

A backwater now
a suburb pitched on the edge of town
scene of outings on the *chinampas*
for the tourists and locals
thronging the gondolas

A little boat punts by
laden with pot plants for sale –
an unsteady *Washingtonia*
fans open its one pale palm
in surrender

TROTSKY'S GARDEN

I wanted to stay in Trotsky's garden,
to sit out the hot day
under the banyan tree,

to find names for the cacti and climbers and shrubs –
the Siberian irises over, cut back for the year,
the scarlet banana

a lit fountain of gold in the sun,
the neat disciplined lawn with its long snaking hose
coiled in the afternoon heat.

I wanted to stay here till sunset,
to witness the sun
as it skirted the walls to pace out the garden,

to feel night closing in,
the huge pull of the city heaving and teeming,
the life of the city as remote as the stars.

★

When Lev Davidovitch
fled to Mexico
with Stalin's dogs snapping at his heels,

he fetched up here –
in this *little fortress* in Coyoacán,
the *zone of coyotes* as it's known to the Aztecs.

The suite of small rooms, half-walled with glass,
is left as he left it.
His old straw sombrero, his walking stick, tossed

on the iron-framed bed;
a fleet of black typewriters on bare wooden desks;
a wall map of Mexico;

yellowing pamphlets in Russian,
in Spanish, in English, in French;
mismatched china and earthenware crockery

and a caddy of Queen Mary tea
in the doll's house-sized kitchen.
His passionate library locked up for good.

★

Nothing else can survive under such harsh conditions:
the absolute zero of night in the desert,
the searing cauldron of noon.

Leaves abandoned for spines and needles.
Fertile soil scorned.
Cocoons of white hair.

Moisture lured from the air
and laid down in sacs,
plumped tissues swollen and secret and viscous.

Columns and barrels and disjointed joints,
taller than palaces
or less than a pebble.

And the absolute triumph of glorious blossoms
cast off at dusk
when no one's to notice —

cerise, tangerine, scarlet, chrome yellow —
the shocking waxed petals flare out of nowhere,
hyperreal, burning and utterly still.

★

Because now there's nothing to be done
but wait for bad news to turn worse,
for the worst to come true —

20

L.D.'s absorbed by his cacti collection,
furtively culled in raids staged at midnight,
while his guards

cock their weapons and scan the horizon.
Look, here he comes
over the brow of the hill for the very last time,

the moon breaking clear of the clouds –
triumphant, filthy, and happy as Larry,
wrestling a huge blue agave back to the car;

big fists of soil thump the ground as he walks,
his face lit up,
a pickaxe slung under one arm.

ZAATAR

for Zakaria Mohammed

Astringent, aromatic, antiseptic –
the souls of the dead
come to rest in the blooms
of this bitter herb

to haunt the bleached landscape
of limestone
of broken stones
of olive trees stricken and wasted

Incendiary – a volatile oil
can be crushed from its leaves
small pockets of scent
toughened, hirsute

Uprooted, exploded
ground under foot
its pungency rises
staining the air –

pollen like gunpowder
dust in the hand
cast over Palestine
from the mouths of stones

COLCHICUM (THE AUTUMN CROCUS)

Shivering in September
    they come out of nowhere –

ghost-blooms –
    their slim flames flaring

in the shrubbery
    at dusk.

Petals the exact shade of pink
    bred under fingernails,

or the mauve of a bruise
    pressed on pale flesh,

or the dead-white of milk teeth
    tucked close to the bone.

Flayed by the rain,
    in October

they are litter –
    ruined things

splayed amongst the leaf-mould,
    the heavy petals

all keeled over,
    their etiolated stems

flat out at random.
    The rot sets in –

dark spots foxing
    the torn inflorescence,

the whole border gone.
    I could talk to you

of resurrection,
    of fat corms fattening

overwinter in the dark,
    of the long straps of leaves

which unwind, unremarked,
    in the spring, on their own –

but not now.
    This is the time for grief,

to look carefully at loss,
    then turn away.

WATERSHED

Overnight, *Bellis perennis*
would heave its fist of leaves
up into the light
rupturing the bowling green.

In the flat heat of the afternoon
I knelt in my small shadow
puncturing the hard earth
with a dining fork,

attempting to unseat
the urchin daisy from its home,
its nude roots woven in the soil,
the pink-flushed blooms

slim embryos, packed within
the tight-whorled leaves;
then I tucked the new seeds in
to mend the wounded soil.

This was the summer
when you could fill your palm
with grass seeds
and I'd know their names:

Festuca rubra commutata
(Chewing's fescue)
Festuca rubra rubra
(strong creeping red)

and *Agrostis tenuis*,
its gentle growth as fine
as baby's hair.
It never rained.

The longest drought since
records began. All July
the tight sky banged above us
all day long.

My reddened shoulders
turned to skin; detached;
a loose, translucent parchment
that streamed off,

frayed, and blossomed
in my twisted sheets
as dust. At work
I learned to use

the Ransomes Auto-Certes;
each week my boss would tinker
with it upside down,
tickling the carburettor,

feeding slips of cartridge paper
into the hive of sharpened blades
until it sliced them
into perfect squares.

Three times
he let me carve the lawn
into its warp and weft,
the shaven grass striped green,

then lighter green,
then green again.
No girl has ever done that,
he told me, when I stopped for tea.

Some of the Bowling Club
are blaming you for this –
he gestured at the sickening lawn.
My sex could blight

their turf. Turn milk
foetid in an hour.
It never rained. By August
we were mowing down the soil.

We gave up watering after eight:
the moisture either dropped
straight through the ground,
or simply turned to steam;

so I rose at four,
watched Venus slip
behind a block of flats,
and left for work.

The dawn released the fragrance
of the lime-flower trees
which cloaked the long,
cool avenue I walked along;

the half-light lifted,
the distant trees, the lawns,
first grey, then glaucous;
the bowling green,

the porter's lodge now
breaking into form.
It never rained. I learned
the fungal sicknesses

of turf by heart:
Fairy Rings, Fusarium patch
(its pink mycelia
like cotton wool)

and red thread
(corticum disease);
in the half-light
of the musty shed

gleamed poisonous tins
of malachite green
to wipe them out.
The *Salix tortuosa*

lost its leaves and died;
its twisted branches
made an absent *haiku*
against the naked wall.

Only the giant hogweed
thrived, spawning
by the putrid riverbank,
its bloated umbels

carried twelve-foot high
by hollow stems
hairy and maculate,
harbouring a vicious juice,

cousin to the hemlock
and to cowbane, to the deadly
hemlock water dropwort.
It never rained.

Each night at home
I found the small rooms
stiff with heat,
the hard air

tight against the glass.
I was nineteen. Waiting
for the sky to open.
I washed my shirt

and watched it dry
from navy into sapphire
in an afternoon.
Across the estate

two dogs were fighting.
I heard the ice-cream van,
the children I no longer
recognised clamouring

outside the flats.
No one called all weekend.
I slept through Sunday.
That night I climbed

the ten flights to the roof
and out onto the flat
expanse of asphalt.
It warmed my back.

I had never seen
so many stars,
so old, so far away,
shining down

their messages of light
from centuries ago.
I didn't know
the constellations,

I lacked the skill
to make the stars reveal
their names and myths –
until one

slid then hurtled
down the sky. Next day
the floods came down.

The long stretch till lunch
after the miles
back from tea-break,

mist cured away
by the bald, implacable sun
– and nothing but tasks,

tasks, in this factory of trees
which are not trees
(*Aesculus, Tilia,*

Ulmus, Acacia)
but tagged products
notched down

the poisoned clay road,
template of rank
and infinity.

Raffia balled in one pocket,
the hard knife hasped
shut in my fist,

I must ship up this pickaxe,
arc it
down in cold clay

till my spine is a fine blade
of fire
and both palms

sting in the morning air,
as I stretch up
to catch

the reinforced windows
of John Conolly's crenellated
Hanwell Asylum,

as in turn I'm surveyed
by a whey-faced crocodile
of long-term patients

gingerly tracing
Brunel's redundant
Grand Union Canal

before lock-up. Before lunch.

Today the day is mainly night,
midday stained with the sump

of darkness,
light laden grey.

By closing time
the park's deserted;

hardwood of the dedicated benches
sodden,

blackened, and rimed with frost.
The yew trees are passing

their parcels of darkness,
furled in small tines;

it seeps from their arms
as the lawn melts away;

little berries
little lanterns

scarlet and deadly
starring the dusk;

the motley *Aucuba* aghast
by the gate.

Fox gone to ground.
Thin flint pebbles

gibber down the long clay path
lined with leafless limetrees,

with wasting grass.
Not a soul.

Only the frozen roar of London
domed under clouds.

MY GRAFTING KNIFE

A whole week's wages
balanced on my palm

The cherrywood clasp
burnished and finished with brass

Lockjaw
I unjoint the heart

and the steel heart
arcs

from silver to blue
hurting the air

The fine blade cleaves
to the whetstone

first a dry rasp grates
the granular carborundum

then the whispered finesse
of the oilstone filmed with oil

Six strops on the leather strap
I could carve

scarves of gossamer tissue
One poised gesture

and the ichor oozes
The knife stop – my right thumb

crisscrossed with hair-scars
tarnished with sap

NO. 3 GREENHOUSE, 7.30 A.M.

Genuflect
crossing the threshold

The unopened air
heady with the odours
of cloves and roses

The carnations are speechless
Candles
ascending the nave

(So easy to befuddle –
remember ink in the jam jar
the pinked frills taking blue)

They must lose their heads
before they turn spray

I stub out the buds
A twist and they're single

Auxins surge from the one heady flower
the bouquet's darling

Cloistered in glass
I am taken by ritual
postulant to the blooms

THE GROWING ROOM

Lux eterna:
the Dutch lamps
beam all night

Walls of loam
shelved in green trays

Dicotyledons
breaking the surface

dense as a rainforest
glimpsed from a plane

Begonia seeds
are costlier than gold:

I tweezer open
the cellophane envelope

unhouse the blond dust
inhale

then waft
the precious cirrus

softly
down to earth

THE MIST BENCH

Even at night, at random
a click
– and mist fumes

from the watchtowers
clouding the cuttings
with fog

Bare leaves are downy
turn blurred
and glaucous

as the fine fur plumps
and sleeves itself
with water

Ten beats and it's
finished
The electric leaf

buried in the leaves
is parched
and replenished

all night

YEAR-ROUND CHRYSANTHEMUMS

In mid-July
they think it is winter

All it takes
is an hour's incandescence

at midnight
and their day

bifurcates: twenty-four hours
makes two

Year-round chrysanthemums
the long nights

make you rich
and fecund

Your bunched, curled faces
magenta and saffron

phototropic with desire
inexorably riding the light

THE COOL FERNERY

Propped in the shadow
of the far west wall
the white-framed windows

are starting to sag –
a nursery for moss
for lichens furring the glass

The ferns release their fronds
in a weather of their own creation –
cool, clear, and utterly still

Tight little fiddleheads
of adder's tongue and moonwort
cast off their veils of silvered fur

and ease their rust into green –
while the arc of the *Osmundia*
describe the perfect parabola of grace

Stowed in the corner
in a dark cupboard built of glass
berthed under glass

are the filmy ferns –
feathery and sodden,
a cell's-breadth of spores and sporangia

They breathe their own mist
and fog up the panes
drunk on dew

THE WARDIAN CASE

Medicines, beverages, crops
all succoured in a small hut
cast half across the world

A glass ark lashed to the deck
A balsawood tabernacle
tucked under the awning

Buoyant
alight
and filled with live wonders

THE GARDEN OF THE VIRGIN

In the Gospel of the Egyptians . . . the Saviour himself said,
I am come to destroy the works of the female.

Clement of Alexandria *Stromateis* Book III

I

Fearing the approach of his second death,
Lazarus – he who had known the chill
of the tomb, who had felt the soft worms
weld to his flesh – Lazarus, the Bishop of Cyprus,
requested the Virgin's blessing. He sent
a boat for her, and Mary sailed from the coast
of Palestine – the clear sky big with itself,
the sea blue as the sky – till a storm drove
her off course, and she came upon her garden.

II

From the far northern coast
of Greece, from the low
treeless shore of Halkidiki,
three arms of land slide into
the Aegean Sea.

From the edge of the third
Mount Athos pierces the sky,
its darkening, gashed
escarpments finished by
a crest of white.

Below, the isthmus falls away,
its rough spine a wood as dense
as any fairy-tale, as thick
with wolves. The forest of Athos
is pungent

with the gums and oils of pine,
of juniper and thuja, is massed
with ilex and arbutus,
with the loose mauve flowers
of the Judas tree.

III

At Clementos, Mary
alighted
into recognition.
The Pagans fled.

In their makeshift
shrines, the idols
of their female gods
debased themselves

before her, imploding
into dust. The Virgin
walked through Athos
in the cool of evening,

inhaling its aromas,
gathering the blooms
of oleander and hibiscus.
She declared this garden

her domain, declared
(recalling Eve)
no other female
should come to foul

this paradise.
Then she left for Cyprus,
for the final death
of Lazarus.

IV

The monks who came to cultivate
the Virgin's garden
obeyed her law.

St Theodosius the Studite wrote:
Keep no female animal
for use in house or field:

the holy fathers
never used such –
nor does nature need them.

Ewelambs and their ewes
were slaughtered. Cows
butchered. Heifers slain.

The sow, the gilt
and the nanny goat:
all dead and banned.

Bitches murdered one
by one. Each hen
felt the press of thumbs

about her throat, the neck
snapped taut – and then
the slump. Each egg

was gathered up, each eggshell
crumpled in a viscid mess of yolk,
thrown oozing down the cliffs,

where, boiling in the waves,
it made a salty broth
the gulls sucked up.

Only the cats stayed on:
the cats to catch the rats
that dropped their young

despite the monks,
despite the Virgin's stern
injunction. At night

it was the cats
who ran the place:
softening the hands and throats

of anchorites and cenobites,
their lithe fur
soothing the flesh made stiff

through deprivation.
And at night the wolves
roamed yowling

through the Virgin's garden:
the sole beast
with cunning enough

to breach the fine neck
of the isthmus.
Miles up, alone

in his stone cottage,
reached only by chains
hung over cliffs,

a hermit wakes up, sodden
from a lycanthropic nightmare,
with his hair

on end. He had sensed
the slow breath
of the wolf, had stared

deep into her lemon eyes,
as still as oil
or candlelight, then

felt himself run off with her –
feral, hirsute, opening out his lungs
to greet the moon.

NOTES

Umbellularia californica

The Californian laurel, or headache tree, gets its common name from the pungent aroma released by crushing its leaves; opinion is divided as to whether the smell actually causes headaches or relieves them. Herbalists use the leaves as an analgesic (painkiller) and a demulcent (a drug soothing to the alimentary canal). The plant was introduced to Britain by David Douglas in 1826. This particular tree lives in the Japanese Garden in Holland Park.

Jasmine in Yemen

A *djambia* is a heavily ornamented – and extremely sharp – curved dagger worn by Yemeni men. The leaves of the *qat* shrub (*Catha edulis*) are mildly narcotic. Chewing *qat* is the most important symbol of Yemeni identity and the entire country seems to come to a halt in the afternoons when everyone retires to chew together. The pleasurable effects of *qat* are achieved by prolonged chewing of the leaves which are kept in one cheek for as long as possible, thus making many Yemenis look like lopsided versions of Dizzy Gillespie.

Chinampas

The canals and 'floating gardens', or *chinampas*, of Xochimilco are what Mexico City (Tenochtitlán) looked like at the time of the Spanish invasion.

Trotsky's Garden

After twelve years on the run from Stalin, Leon Trotsky finally found refuge in Mexico in 1937. In 1939 he moved into the 'little fortress' at Viena 45 in Coyoacán, a quiet suburb of Mexico City, where he was fatally attacked on 20 August 1940. While in Mexico he became a keen gardener and developed a passion for collecting cacti. See Isaac Deutscher, *The Prophet Outcast: Trotsky 1929–1940* (Oxford, O.U.P.; 1963) p.448. Strictly speaking, an agave is a succulent not a cactus.

Zaatar

Zaatar is the Arabic word for thyme (*Thymus vulgaris*) and is the plant most powerfully associated with Palestine, where it grows in profusion.

The Tree Bank at Ten

The London Borough of Ealing's Tree Bank is situated on a strip of wasteland just outside Southall, west London, between the Great Western Railway and the Grand Union Canal. John Conolly (1794–1866), the most important early Victorian psychiatrist, was responsible for introducing a benign and humane regime to the large public Hanwell Asylum during his period as superintendent there between 1839 and 1844. The old building still stands and, during the time the poem is set (1974–7, when I was an apprentice gardener with the Ealing Parks' Department) it was known as St Bernard's psychiatric hospital.

The Wardian Case

A small, portable glasshouse, the Wardian case was devised by Nathaniel Bagshaw Ward in 1830 at Chelsea Physic Garden, utilising the thin sheet-glass recently developed by Joseph Paxton at Chatsworth. As well as playing a big part in the Victorian fern craze, the Wardian case permitted the transfer of commercial crops such as tea from China to India, quinine from South America to India, and rubber to Malaya from South America. An example can be found in the Cool Fernery at Chelsea.